Sunshine —
Hope you enjoy the book,

I
Choose
Life

—

I WANT TO LIVE

by
Scott Houchin

CARDIAC BOOKS

I Choose Life: I Want To Live.

THIS BOOK IS DEDICATED...

To my family that I miss so much.

To Sharyn, who took care of me.

To my many friends who helped me write this book.

To climbers and bicyclists everywhere: stay safe!

And to my patients — especially stroke and

traumatic brain injury survivors worldwide.

This book is for you.

I know it is a struggle, but live your life.

You are not alone!

Contents

ACKNOWLEDGMENTS

There are many people who helped me write this book, but none is more important than my friend and therapist Anne Grasee. She became my therapist a few months after my fall on the Grand Teton and she remained my therapist until her death in November 2017. She was a constant source of encouragement, urging me to write this book. More simply put: this book would not have been written if not for her support and encouragement. Thank you, Anne. You are missed!

CHAPTER 1

Waking Up

It's blurry. I'm being helped to walk. I'm in some sort of facility. The painted walls and the smell — an institution.

It takes a few moments for me to realize I'm not being helped to walk — I'm being helped into a wheelchair by two young men in uniforms.

"What happened?"

"Do you remember your accident?" they ask.

"What accident"?

I'd had a mountain climbing accident, they tell me.

I deny this: "I did NOT have a climbing accident!"

And I'm back in the cloud.

Next memory: lying in bed. My stepmother Beverly and my friend Sharyn are in the room. Daylight. I ask Beverly, "Where's Dad"?

"Don't you remember"? she says.

Then I'm back in the cloud.

The pain. I hurt horribly. Weeks on Tylenol with codeine cause "some issues" with digestion and constipation. The pain is so bad it brings me out of the cloud.

A procedure is done, then I'm back in the cloud.

§

A few mornings later I'm talking to Sharyn and my doctors. Finally I realize I've been in a cloud. I remember that Dad died several years ago. I remember climbing the Grand Teton. I remember hiking down the mountain and putting my weight on a rock.

And that is the last thing I remembered until I was helped into the wheelchair.

It's September. I was climbing the Grand in mid-August. I've been unconscious for over three weeks, but now I'm out of the cloud.

Little do I realize that being in the cloud is the easy part.

CHAPTER 2

The Grand Tetons

The Grand Tetons have always been a special place for me. My best family memories are from there.

My father was a doctor in a small rural farm town in the South. I was raised in a time when doctors still made house calls and delivered babies in people's homes. This sounds like a John-Boy Walton fantasy. In reality, it meant that my father was hardly ever home. He was on the road, making a house call, delivering a baby (most of my classmates were delivered by my dad); doing rounds at the hospital or at his office. He was rarely home and when he was home, he was exhausted. I only saw my dad on vacations.

My family's favorite vacation was the Grand Tetons. It was the one time we were a family and it lasted for a week or so. It was the one time we were "the Houchins." During this whole vacation gig we were together 24/7. We were a family. We were a unit. We knew who we were, why we were here (on earth) and where we were going. I loved it!

When we visited the Tetons, we'd stay in a log cabin on Jackson Lake. In the mornings, my mom would cook Canadian bacon, eggs and potatoes. I can still taste that Canadian bacon. She would cook outside right by the lake on a Coleman stove. It was a national park, so hunting was not allowed, and sometimes deer would be grazing nearby. My sister Pat and I would go down to Jackson Lake and throw rocks at the oil drum barrels that were used to mark off the swimming area in the lake. The beach was filled with millions of rocks that fit perfectly in your hand. The first day both Pat and I would have sore arms and shoulders from throwing rocks at the drums. By Day Three we were pros.

Directly across the lake from where we were throwing rocks was one of the most beautiful scenes in North America: the entire Teton Range. Even as a child, I was drawn to climb those mountains.

I Choose Life

I was a teenager during the Sixties, and like most Americans, the decade had an influence on me and my family and we had our fair share of hardships. The Sixties were a difficult time in America. Folks tend to forget what it was like to have so many assassinations. Then in the early Seventies Nixon "resigned"— that is, was forced from office. It was a very hard time for Americans and my family felt it, just as did most Americans.

My family did not visit the Tetons during the entire Seventies, but I never forgot about them. They were always in my thoughts and that is one of the cool things about mountains: people may change, but the mountains do not.

Mom died in 1980 at a young age and Dad died of leukemia in 1992. Now, in 1995, Sharyn and I were loving life, and she had come to love the Grand Tetons too. We had both climbed the Middle Teton together a few years earlier and we had some vacation time. So we packed up the car, left Denver and headed for the Tetons.

CHAPTER 3

Climbing

Why climb the Grand Teton? If you have ever seen the Grand Teton in person, you would not ask that question. If you have not seen the Grand up close and personal, then there is no use in trying to use words to describe it. Look at a photo of the Grand. Or better yet, just re-look at photos because you have already seen photos of the Grand and probably did not even know it. It is in countless movies, photos, Christmas cards and advertisements.

If you have ever stood at Jackson Lake, then you would know exactly why I wanted to climb the Grand. In fact, the first time I ever thought of ever climbing anything I was looking at the Grand.

I Choose Life

I have always been drawn to the mountains. My first love was the Tetons. However, soon after the Tetons I fell in love with The Smokies, in Gatlinburg, Tennessee. They were also a place my parent frequently took my sister and me on vacation and when I got older, I lived there for a few years as a hippie. Living there for a long period of time sealed the deal. I loved the Smokies. The rivers, the huge trees, the forest floor all fascinated me, and then there were the animals and the fish. Walking through a deep mountain forest, I felt as though time had stopped. It was enchantment.

I learned to climb in New England. I was a civil rights investigator in Kentucky and I applied for a job doing civil rights in Boston and I got it. When I got there, I immediately joined the Appalachian Mountain Club and started taking trips up to Pinkham Notch at the base of Mount Washington in New Hampshire. Being from the South, I had never been in snow like they have in the White Mountains. I remember one of my first cross country ski trips out of Pinkham and the snow came up to my waist. Unbelievable!

Cross country ski trips and hiking trips turned into mountain climbing trips up Mt. Washington. I then moved on to ice climbing and the deal was done. I was officially hooked. I became involved with Sharyn in Boston and we both loved the mountains and hiking.

Boston is a very expensive town to live in and I transferred to the Denver office doing civil rights. When we moved to Denver we both joined the Colorado Mountain Club (CMC) and our weekends were filled with our hiking and cross-country ski trips. On my own, I became a (volunteer) climbing instructor with the Boulder CMC and I was pretty good at it. Ice climbing became my specialty.

During the whole time I was learning how to climb, I never forgot about the Tetons. Some of my best life memories were of me standing on the beach at Jackson Lake gazing across at the Teton Range. The mountains absolutely grip you. If you can look at the Grand Tetons and not feel the seduction to climb them, then you are a better (or worse) person than me. Now that I was a climber, I knew that I would come back to my beloved Tetons and climb them.

The Middle Teton, just to the southwest of The Grand Teton, is the first Teton Sharyn and I climbed. It was a scary ordeal. We were the only ones climbing at the time; there wasn't even anyone else at the Meadows camping area below us. A mix of rain and snow was falling. And we were up in the clouds.

Lightning is not a joke to mountain climbers. It can kill in a heartbeat. Our climb was not a "technical climb" — that is, it wasn't a climb that required special mountaineering equipment — but it was very difficult. We both realized that a wrong move could mean serious injury.

But we did climb it without incident. And now I found myself wanting to climb the Grand.

Sharyn and I were getting financially comfortable, so we made arrangements with the major mountain guide outfit that led expeditions up The Grand: Exum Guides. I would make the two-day climb up The Grand; Sharyn would do some other hikes around the lakes. We drove to the Exum office; I signed the necessary documents and gave them the money. Then I shook everyone's hand, and Sharyn and I said our good-byes. There was nothing left to do but go climb the Grand Teton.

My climbing group headed out.

CHAPTER 4

The Climb

We were slogging up the trail. The climb up The Grand is a long hike. On the first day, hikers climb in altitude more than 5,000 feet.

We had young people in our group — maybe 12 years old or so. Their gait was slow since their legs were shorter than ours. We took maybe one step for every two steps they took. So we spent lots of time on the trail.

I talked to our guide a fair amount. I explained that I was a climbing instructor with the Colorado Mountain Club and that my specialty was ice climbing. I also explained that part of my purpose for my climb was to scout the Black Ice Couloir Route.

The Black Ice Couloir — a "couloir" is a crevice — is probably the Grand Teton's most famous ice climb. It has a reputation of being a good "mixed climb" — both rock and ice climbing. This was the type of climbing I liked and I felt that it would be the sort of ice climb I'd be comfortable leading. So I planned on checking it out on my way down to get a good look at it.

I'd read that in recent years this couloir has melted out and reformed more than once. And the guide said she wasn't sure what sort of condition it was in, since it was mid-August, but she thought it was probably still in shape to climb. I explained to her that I hadn't planned to climb it on this trip and that I only had time to climb The Grand — and besides, I hadn't bought my ice gear, which is specialized, and necessary for a climb like the Black Ice Couloir.

We walked on together a little further. I told her I really enjoyed teaching folks how to ice climb; that most novices think that the real work is swinging the ice axe, but that once I showed them how to use their crampons to kick into the ice without shattering it, they began to learn that for all but overhanging ice, the footwork is the key to ice climbing. She reminded me that she had never been ice climbing and didn't really know what I was talking about.

A few more steps along, she added, "You might be interested to know that one of the best ice climbers in the world is walking in the group in front of us." I looked ahead and could see another group of Exum climbers and students — about ten or so. They were about 150 feet ahead of us. But I didn't recognize anyone, and no one really stuck out that much. So I asked who it might be.

"Alex Lowe," she said.

I knew the name instantly. Alex Lowe is not "one of the best"; he is considered the very best ice climber in the world by just about every climbing magazine, climbing writer and gear freak. I'd frequently read about him. He was a legend within the ice-climbing community. My guide said that sometimes — Alex would come to Exum to make some money for the next climb, and that he was here helping out today.

I walked on, not sure how to respond to her comment. It was like playing a round of golf and seeing Tiger Woods walk up to my partner and start chatting about the weather. Or — if you are into politics — it would be like going to a routine Democratic fundraiser and having Bill Clinton walk up and say hello to the people you are hanging out with. I guess maybe a step

13

higher, since it was Alex Lowe. Maybe it would be like having Bill Clinton and Monica walk up together and start chit chatting. Even better if he comments to Monica, "Hey Monica, I think it is about time to get that dress cleaned," which of course would have meant it was a game-changing moment in world history. Well, maybe not that important — but Alex Lowe was and is still known as possibly the world's best ice climber.

I had absolutely no idea what to say. I finally just said, "Alex Lowe is one of the best ice climbers in the world!" She said, "I know."

Another 30 steps. "Do you think I will have a chance to shake his hand?"

"Of course. He's staying at the Exum Hut tonight," she replied, referring to the "hut" in the lower saddle between the Grand and Middle Teton where those of us in the Exum groups would be staying overnight.

I almost fell down! I knew that world-class climbers frequently worked at guiding companies here and in Yosemite to fund their next trip — or even just for fun. However, this morning when I signed up to climb the Grand, I was not expecting to meet Alex Lowe.

§

I met him sooner than expected. An afternoon "crack and boom" thunderstorm on the mountain had our guides herding us under huge boulders that formed kind of a cave. We were well protected from the pouring rain (which lasted all of 15 minutes) and during that time, as we all sat huddled together in our shelter, I took the time to introduce myself to Alex and tell him what an honor it was to meet a climber of his caliber.

Alex, who had a reputation of being a climber's climber as well as an all-round nice guy, just smiled, thanked me, and asked me the sort of questions a celebrity climber trying to be polite would ask a novice: "How long have you been ice climbing?" "Where do you usually climb?" "Have you done any ice climbs on the Grand?" I did respond to that one, telling him I was hoping to scout the Black Ice Couloir while up on the Grand. He said it was a fun climb, a good mixed — climb, of both ice and rock climbing.

I do not know if Alex had anything to do with my rescue after my fall. His group was on top about the same time as my group. I don't remember seeing Alex on top before my accident, but it was a real reward to meet such an unassuming international climber of such talent and experience.

15

I Choose Life

As they say, "There are old climbers and bold climbers, but there are no old, bold climbers." When you climb world-class mountains, even when you do everything correctly, you still have only about 30 percent control over what happens to you on the mountain. Alex was the perfect example of this. He had been doing everything correct on mountains for so long that he probably did everything correct without even realizing it. But a few years after I fell, Alex was on Shishapangma in Tibet and a huge avalanche broke loose. It was a fluke, but I imagine Alex probably had time to realize "This is it" before the avalanche swallowed and killed him.

I am sure that Alex was doing everything we think is correct and safe in mountaineering. However, even when you are the best, you still have minimal control over what happens. The rest is simply fate, or what we call fate, for lack of a better word or explanation. Whatever it is, it is what happened to Alex Lowe on that day on Shishapangma in Tibet.

§

Back on the trail, after the afternoon rainstorm, we hiked up to the lower saddle between the Middle Teton and Grand Teton where the Exum Camp is located. Sleeping at altitudes over 10,000 feet is never pleasant, and the Exum Camp is at 11,600 feet. I will not go into a 5,000-word explanation of altitude; I will simply say that sleeping at altitude is never easy. Even if you have just hiked 5 to 6 miles and climbed 5,000 feet that day, such a hike tends to energize the body so much that even without the altitude gain it would be difficult to sleep. But the food was good, and the hut protected us from the wind, rain, and chill.

We woke at 4 a.m. the next morning, put on our helmets, and started climbing in pitch black, with just the stars for light. Some climbers hadn't brought headlamps, so the guides would not let any of us use our headlamps, because they tend to blind folks that do not have any sort of light device. Without light it was slow going! But within an hour or so the sun started coming up and it looked to be a beautiful day.

We hiked up to the point where some "technical climbing" was required, so we put on our harnesses, distributed the rock climbing protection, and roped up. It was not a difficult rock climb. We were on top within a couple of hours.

"Sitting on top of the world" does not accurately describe what it is like up there. I have climbed a lot of hills and many were higher than the Grand's 13,000+ feet, but usually there are other peaks around that are close and as high, or higher. Not so here. The Grand Teton was the highest point as far as the eye could see.

The weather was good, so we had some time to mess around. I broke from the group and went off by myself. As I have mentioned, the Grand Teton National Park was where I felt the closest to my family. I sought some privacy for some personal moments thinking of my mother and father. They had both died, and part of the reason I had climbed the Grand was to honor their memories and the memory of my family, since this is where some of my best memories of them were. It seemed fitting. A few moments of silence and meditation, and I was back on top with the others.

Lots of photos, and then, although we had good weather, there was no reason to push our luck, so we started down. After about 30 minutes, my guide pointed out the Black Ice Couloir, to our right. She knew I wanted to look at it.

I carefully walked over to the top of the climb. It was a couloir, a narrow gully with a steep decline. I could tell it would be a beautiful climb. The ice looked at least a couple of inches thick on much of the route and it was at least a foot wide; in many places the ice looked to be 3 feet wide or more. The rock formations on both sides of the couloir would provide plenty of protection. It was a good rock and ice mixed climb, which was my favorite! It also looked to be within my skill set. I looked forward to coming back to the Grand and doing this one. Probably I would bring a group of trusted CMC buddies, and I'd just lead it and not use a guide.

We continued down. We had climbed over 5,000 feet up the previous day, and now we were going to climb all the way down to our cars today. We were tired!

We came to a place where the decline increased dramatically. The very steep slope made me nervous. The guides asked if we wanted to rope up. I started to say "yes," because as a climbing instructor for the CMC, I certainly would have roped up my climbers for a downhill climb like this. However, nobody said they wanted to be roped up. In fact, quite the opposite. Most felt they could easily handle it. So I bit my lip and we started down. I was still nervous and at one point I saw I had to step down in an uncomfortable way. So I steadied myself by grabbing onto a large rock that was waist/shoulder high and put my weight on it as I started to climb down.

The next thing I remember is being helped into the wheelchair – three weeks later.

I Choose Life

I have been told that when I grabbed onto and put my weight on the rock, which was "half the size of a refrigerator," it simply pulled out of the mountain and hit me in the head. Then I rolled and tumbled for approximately 100 feet and landed on a ledge. According to the guides, if I had gone off the ledge, I would not be alive to be writing this story.

The even worse part of this story is that when I went flying as the rock pulled loose, I hit another climber squarely, and he then also went rolling and tumbling down the steep slope. He and I both stopped on the ledge. If either of us had gone off the ledge, we would have died because it was a long, 90-degree vertical drop.

I did not know the climber I fell on, but I did see him while we were on top of the Teton. He was also with an Exum guided group.

He lived! So did I!

The day we fell was August 22, 1995.

CHAPTER 5

The Cloud

No, I did not see a light at the end of the tunnel. Several people have asked me that question. Unfortunately, or maybe fortunately, when I was in the cloud I did not see, hear, or feel anything. The cloud was no memory of anything. Nothing.

Going into the cloud, and coming out of the cloud: that was a different thing altogether. But during the three weeks when I was in the cloud directly after my accident, nothing.

Medically the cloud was "post traumatic amnesia." It has been explained to me that when you are in this state your brain is simply not recording. Anything.

I Choose Life

So you have no memory of anything. In my case, my brain was too swollen. Luckily, I did not burst any major vessels within my skull. No subdural or epidural hematomas. The MRIs showed I had diffused bruising and small lesions all over my brain; extensive swelling — and the swelling is why I was in the cloud.

According to other climbers at the accident site, I was unconscious for about five minutes, which in the EMT world is no small potatoes. Five minutes is usually a sign of a significant traumatic brain injury (TBI), which I had. After I became conscious, the standard "alert and oriented" (A & O) questions were asked: "What is your name? Do you know where you are? What day is it? Who is the president? Do you remember what happened?"

I could only remember who I was, which was classified "A&O X1". Not very good. Although my brain was so swollen that it did not record anything, the good news was that my brain stem was not damaged, and was working, so I could digest food, see, talk, breathe, and go to the bathroom. I just had no memory of anything.

Sharyn said the nurses would tell me to leave my cannula (the oxygen device going into my nose) alone and to stop pulling it out, and I would reply, "OK";

then pull it out 30 seconds later and not realize what I had done. I would talk and make no sense. I would remember people's names for about 15 seconds, then forget who they were. I was awake, but I was "not there" — or as they say, "the lights were on, but no one was home." I was not only "not at home"; for the most part, I was not even on the planet. And that was me for about three weeks.

I have already described a few events as I started coming out of the cloud and becoming Scott again. But those events I described at the start of the book actually took place over several days. I would have only moments outside the cloud; then I would go back into the cloud.

To be quite honest about it, I wanted back in the cloud. My brain was totally exhausted — literally. I wasn't tired the way you'd be after a 50-mile bike ride; no, I was mentally exhausted, which is different and much worse than just being "tired". The act of seeing — sight — probably requires more mental energy than any of the other senses. I could only "see" what was going on around me for a few minutes, and then my brain's energy was all used up, and I would just fall back asleep in the cloud. Actually, "falling asleep" or "drifting back into the cloud" doesn't really do it justice. It is more accurately described as "overpowering mental fatigue". I was not in control of the situation. My brain would just tell me to shut up and close my eyes, and at that point I would immediately go back into the cloud. This went on for months.

In movies, patients "come out of the cloud" — out of a coma or unconsciousness — and a few minutes later they are carrying on competent and engaging conversations. In real life it's nothing remotely like that. It took me months to fully come out of the cloud. My brain was protecting me. It would not let me out of the cloud but for small amounts of time.

There's new focus today on concussions and sports. As EMTs, we learn about these things, since we are the ones treating the players on the field. The new medical science about this condition goes into depth about the brain's need to recover. We learn it takes weeks, not hours, of rest after an injury for the brain to recover. If the brain does not get enough rest, it does not recover correctly. Then the next blow is much worse — much, much worse. Then, a third injury.

This is why there are tens of millions of dollars tied up in court cases regarding concussions and sports.

CHAPTER 6

Treatment

I woke up in Idaho. I'd been sent there from Jackson because there was a good head injury unit in Idaho Falls, Idaho. It was there that I finally realized that I was still alive, that I had a serious brain injury.

My TBI was only one of my injuries. I had a considerable number of injuries. The talus bone in my left ankle was broken, and I'd severely sprained my right ankle; thus, I could not walk at all. My right wrist was broken in several places. I had a collapsed lung. And I had deep bruising all over my back and abdomen. It was true: I was a train wreck.

The talus bone is a particularly bad bone to break.

Circulation is an issue with this kind of break. It was possible the bone would not heal correctly, and my left ankle would have to be fused, so to ensue proper healing, they put pins and screws in into my ankle.

To repair my right wrist, surgeons drilled into my radius bone and wrist and inserted screws at several locations. Then they ran a 3/8-inch-wide pipe between the screws, running the length of my wrist and partially up my arm. It allowed absolutely no movement of my wrist.

By the time I "woke up," the surgeries had been done, much of my bruising had faded and I was breathing as though nothing had happened. But my ability to walk again — much less hike or ski — was very much up in the air. It would totally depend on how well I healed.

One of my physical therapists took her first look at me and said, "Wow, a train wreck!" then added that she would help me totally recover.

By far the most serious injury was my TBI. As the doctors said, every patient is different — and this is particularly true of head injuries. No one had any real idea how much I would "come back."

While I was given the soft truth, Sharyn was told

the hard truth: that I might not be able to work again; might not be able to drive again — and on and on. I was being tested, repeatedly and often, on my cognitive status. Doctors were worried, for example, that I would be driving and when I came to a red light, that even after driving for a couple weeks successfully, this time I'd not make the connection that I should stop; that I'd run the light and get seriously hurt or injure others — not to mention the legal and civil consequences for me and the doctors who'd given me the OK to drive. So, I was constantly under scrutiny and being tested for cognitive abilities. My recovery would all depend on how much I "came back".

It was time to go back to Colorado for rehab. Sharyn was an attorney and she knew how to make things happen. She arranged for me to be flown from Idaho to Denver by a medical transport twin prop plane over the Continental Divide down to Denver. I was sedated, but Sharyn later said the ride was "interesting". In other words, scary. Apparently, many of the mountains were too high for the little plane to fly over, so we flew in between then. She described it as a white-knuckle event. All I knew about the trip at the time was that I slept well.

In Denver I was admitted to the brain injury ward of a rehabilitation facility. Sharyn had arranged for me to have a private room with a TV and DVD player.

Day and night, for weeks, there was nothing but Physical Therapy (PT), Occupational Therapy (OT), Speech Therapy (ST), testing, more testing, and shrink session after shrink session. Sleep was sandwiched in between. My day went something like this: wake up and get helped into my chair. Go down to breakfast and come back to my room. Then a session of PT. Back to my room to sleep for thirty minutes. Then an OT session. Then more sleep. Then lunch and then a nap. Next a shrink session, then ST or OT. Back to my room to sleep. Then it was dinnertime. They'd wheel me down to the cafeteria for dinner, but for once in my life I did not feel like eating. It was not that the food was not good; it was just that I simply did not feel like eating. Fortunately, Sharyn was at dinner with me, and she would make me eat. That is, she'd sit with me and encourage me to eat.

Weeks went by before I started getting my appetite back. Those that knew me well realized that my appetite coming back signaled that I was getting better. After dinner we'd come back to my room for a couple of hours of watching TV or movies and chit/chat. Then I'd sleep.

And this was my life. Wake up. Some breakfast and

then PT or OT. Then more sleep. Wake up and then more PT/OT/ST and then back to sleep.

Days went by. Then weeks went by and not much changed. At least I did not think much changed. I was constantly being tested, evaluated, and watched by everyone. According to the docs, I was recovering at a very good pace.

They had strategies to bring me back. One strategy that seemed to work well with TBI patients was to play music the patient had listened to prior to their accident. So they used this strategy with me. Two of my favorite artists (besides The Grateful Dead) are Leonard Cohen and Nancy Griffith. So Sharyn bought a tape player and I started listening to them constantly.

This strategy also worked with movies. So, Sharyn brought in a video player and I started watching all the movies I'd really liked before the accident. Something interesting happened with the movie-watching, though: Before my accident I'd liked Arnold Schwarzenegger movies like *The Terminator*. They were popular in the climbing community during the late 80s and early 90s (frequently climbs were even named from Terminator movie content) and I was part of all that. But now when I tried to watch *Terminator*-type movies, I found them to be so violent they were almost boring.

So the search was on for better movies for me to watch. By accident Sharyn found a movie that I became absolutely infatuated with: *Downhill Racer*, starring Robert Redford. It is a movie about skiing, and some of it was filmed in Georgetown and Idaho Springs, Colorado. Both were towns I'd been to many times.

When *Downhill Racer* first came out in the late 60s, I'd watched it at least three times — once in the movie theater and twice at drive-ins.

This movie turned out to be exactly what the doctor ordered: a movie I'd enjoyed in my youth and was able to watch again now, having it bring back all my earlier memories! *Downhill Racer*!

I fell in love with skiing while watching the 1964 Winter Olympics, held in Innsbruck, Austria. Billy Kidd, Jimmy Heuga and Buddy Werner were the USA top male skiers, but American men had never won a medal in alpine skiing. At the time, the sport was dominated by European skiers like Jean Claude Killy. The Americans went into the Olympics as underdogs, but Jimmy Heuga and Billy Kidd won medals — the first time the U. S. men's alpine ski team had won Olympic medals. That was the story told in *Downhill*

Racer.

I think of that time as my "Innsbruck Era." I was thirteen years old, and I became obsessed with skiing — to the point that I forced my mother to buy my sister and me a pair of skis from Canada for $12. There were no ski resorts close to where we lived so the few times it snowed we would ski in cow pastures behind our house. My mom called us the "La Grange Ski Patrol." Other kids in Kentucky were learning how to ride horses, swim, play basketball and football. I wanted to learn how to ski.

Downhill Racer brought all those memories back for me. It was exactly the kind of movie the doctors hoped would help me regain my memory. It worked! *Downhill Racer* probably did it more than any one stimulus to heal my memory.

So this became my routine: wheel myself down to breakfast; PT, OT, ST, shrinks, sleep, wake up and watch some *Downhill Racer* or listen to some Nancy Griffith, then back to sleep. Wake up. Do some PT, then OT, then back to sleep. Maybe a visit from Sharyn, then to supper to try to eat some food, then back to my room. Some socializing, but back to sleep early. If I woke up in the night, I would watch *Downhill Racer* until I became sleepy again.

CHAPTER 7

PTSD

Many people who have had a TBI also have PTSD.

The most important thing to know about Post Traumatic Stress Disorder (PTSD) is that once you have it, you will always have it. There is no cure. There is treatment, and the treatment works — or at least it works to the point that your life becomes acceptable. But once you have PTSD, it is yours for life.

After the Vietnam War, there was such a stigma to having PTSD that many of those who had it would not let anyone know, due to the fear and misunderstanding people had of those with PTSD. When someone (usually a male) revealed that he had PTSD and that he had "flashbacks", he was almost immediately considered dangerous and unpredictable. "PTSD" began to be a label attached to any unexplainable violent behavior, including shootings and murder. The stereotype was that people with PTSD were a time bomb that could go off without warning.

Naturally, this stereotype morphed into discrimination against people with PTSD. People with PTSD — typically men — could not find jobs or were fired from jobs. Landlords refused to rent to them, or evicted them.

As with almost any disability, PTSD delivered a double whammy: First, you had to deal with the disability itself and learn to live with it. Then you had to live with people's fear of your disability.

Probably the biggest number of PTSD victims in our country's history was from yet another war: World War II. The entire world was at war. In America, almost all the World War II soldiers and nurses — those who saw action or witnessed a significant amount of death and horror — came home with some form of PTSD. Back then they called it "battle fatigue" or "shell shock."

Forty to 60 million people were killed in WWII. Hundreds of millions felt the personal trauma of the camps, the war, the bombings with tens of thousands killed in a single night. It is impossible to know how many of them had symptoms of PTSD. It can only be guessed. All of Europe; most of Asia; much of the population in the Pacific suffered the effects. In fact, only North and South America escaped the first-hand carnage of that war.

As for the Americans coming home: those poor guys and gals. There was no treatment for them back then and they were basically ignored. PTSD as a medical condition had not yet been recognized. An entire generation of Americans were walking around the country suffering from it and, as those suffering from PTSD typically do, they tried on their own to become "as normal as possible." Because they knew they were not normal.

Being normal in the 50's meant finding a job, getting married, having kids. Because they felt like "something" was very wrong, people back then who had PTSD tried to fit in as best they could. Today we'd want to call that a form of denial, but it couldn't be denial if no one knew about PTSD.

With no other help to be found, folks with PTSD self-medicated. They used alcohol. It works! Better said, it numbs, and numbing is what the Fifties were all about: becoming as normal as possible and trying to forget the horror of the previous decade of an entire world at war with itself.

I myself have used alcohol to treat my PTSD.

How to explain PTSD? I personally describe it as living through the death experience. If you have been in a situation where you thought you were going to die, or a traumatizing death experience, then probably you have PTSD. I am not talking about almost slipping on the stairs and thinking, "Whew that was close!" or almost stepping in front of a moving truck and again saying, "Whew, that was close!" No, I am talking about an experience where death is imminent, and you can see that are losing your life — or at least you feel like it. You are dying, and you can feel yourself dying. At that moment, the most dreaded fear in humans is released: The fear of death. It is an overpowering and completely dominating fear. It is primal. You feel it the moment you think you are dying or about to die. Primal fear: that is the fear you feel when you have PTSD.

When a PTSD event is "triggered" the patient has a "flashback". Flashbacks are nothing like those film versions with weird music and blurred camera angles. Flashbacks are basically when the primal fear overtakes the person. The fear is so overwhelming that frequently the person cannot understand what is going on. It's all-consuming, and the personality change of someone undergoing a flashback is easily noticeable by others.

I know, because I have PTSD.

Someone experiencing a PTSD flashback doesn't realize the danger they feel is not real, or is not anywhere as alarming as they perceive it as; something that someone without PTSD wouldn't conside at all alarming. When you are having a PTSD "episode" the danger to you seems very real. Others telling you "there is nothing to fear" will likely have little effect; it might just alienate you.

Friends and loved ones of those who have PTSD should be aware that when an episode occurs, it affects the entire patient — all the senses are affected and the fear can easily become overpowering. This is one reason people drink when they have PTSD. Alcohol "numbs" the fear and provides some relief. Having PTSD and becoming dependent on alcohol is not a weakness; for those without proper medicine and training or therapy, drinking is simply the only thing that works. Do not discount this. Unless people with PTSD receive professional treatment, their only relief from the pain is alcohol — or possibly other drugs. However, alcohol usually works best.

Currently there is no cure for PTSD. However, when those of us with the condition are taught how PTSD works — what it does to the mind; how to recognize it; and what to do when it is overpowering us, in other words, with proper counseling and therapy — then we can at least learn how to live with it. I cannot emphasize enough that the fear of imminent death is one of the most powerful primal fears in living creatures. You are not going to stop that fear, but you can learn to recognize what it is, how to make it through episodes, and how to take back control of events. When you are in control, the effects of PTSD tend to dissolve. Recognition is probably the biggest key to unlocking the chain of events. Once you learn to recognize when you are having a PTSD episode, the episode starts to fade away. At least that usually works.

CHAPTER 8

Chris

On May 27, 1995, Christopher Reeve became a quadriplegic after being thrown from a horse during an equestrian competition in Culpeper, Virginia. He required a wheelchair and a portable ventilator for the rest of his life. He lobbied on behalf of people with spinal-cord injuries and for human embryonic stem cell research, founding the Christopher Reeve Foundation and co-founding the Reeve-Irvine Research Center. (*from Wikipedia.*)

Christopher Reeve, the famous "Superman" actor who became a quadriplegic, had his accident a few months before I had mine. The world was horrified when the "Man of Steel" became a quad. As a victim of a fall myself, I tried to seek out any information I could about the man and how he was dealing with his injury.

Reeve became seen as a significant disability advocate — simply due to his fame as the actor who played Superman. Most Americans, besides being shocked, felt sympathy for him. A number of my radical disability rights friends were very uncomfortable with Reeve as a salesman for the disability movement. They felt he didn't really know much about what disabled people needed.

Let me explain:

Reeve, a well-known, well-liked Hollywood actor, was financially quite comfortable. Most disabled people, even those who were well educated and skilled, found that social systems in America simply shut them out. They lived on the edge financially. They dealt daily with incredible hurdles in just about every aspect of their lives: How will I pay my rent? How will I get to the grocery store to buy food (that is, if I have money)? How do I get the bags of food back into my apartment? How do I find an apartment? How do I find a job? How can I get to my job in a wheelchair? How do

I Choose Life

I find a social worker to answer all these questions?

Most of what non-disabled people take for granted disabled people had to figure out and deal with every day just to survive.

The issue at its most basic had to do with money. To the severely disabled person, money can literally mean the difference between life and a casket.

I was very interested in finding out about Reeve both as an advocate and as a disabled person.

As I was lying in my bed one night, one of the news interviews shows — it might have been "Sixty Minutes" or "Frontline" — featured an interview with Reeve. Naturally I paid close attention.

The interview was going well when I heard Reeve say, "It could have been much worse. It could have been a traumatic brain injury."

I lay there stunned at what I had just heard. Lying there in my bed with a prognosis of possibly never walking again; possibly never driving again; possibly never working again or participating in sports; having sex — even as I lay there not knowing whether I would ever be able to again have the life I'd had prior to my accident, I heard Reeve say those words. And I knew he was wrong.

Reeve muttered these words in between taking breaths. It was difficult for him to say the words. I lay there watching him struggle and I felt for him. He was on an assisted breathing machine, and he could not take in that much air through his trach. The process of speaking required letting air out and doing that and then breathing air in through the trach was simply an intricate task, and he was having difficulty with it.

I felt for him. He was trying so hard. I know about trachs. I woke up in a brain injury ward. They locked the doors at night not to keep others out but to keep us in. There were patients in my ward who had injuries like Chris. Many of them were quads with trachs, and many of them were young. They were mostly victims of car and motorcycle accidents, but our ward had people who'd had all kinds of accidents, including beatings and rape. Their struggle was immense. They were fighting just to stay alive. Life for just another month was what many of these patients were striving for. One more month of life was a gift. The term "quality of life" did not seem to come up all that much, except when the insurance people came around.

About Chris's statement regarding TBI: Even with all my injuries I realized that I was not as seriously injured as he was, and I knew my chances for recovery were better than his. They might not be good, but they were better than his and I knew it. I remember thinking that very thing when he made his statements in the interview. It might not have been a nice thing to for me think but I did think it. I also knew it was true.

Later, I would think of that moment and strangely, I would remember reading about soldiers in WWII describing their reaction to comrades who had fallen in combat. Many of the fallen had been good friends. The survivors would say, "But for the grace of God, it would have been me." Then, the ultra-cold reality: "Better him than me."

To this day, I am not sure how much my thought sprang from denial and how much was just plain determination. But when I was in the rehab hospital, not a day went by that I did not think about what Chris had said. As I lay in my bed recalling his words, I'd say out loud, "I choose life! I want to live!

The words I have written above are from Scott the Patient. Now, more than 20 years later, I'm an emergency medical technician, so now I'm on the "patient care" side of the "patient care/patient" relationship. I believe I know now what was going on with Reeve back then. I strongly suspect (or as we say in medicine, "I have a suspicion") that Reeve's doctors were trying to keep alive in Reeve the thing we see as the most crucial key to patient survival: hope.

You do not have to be a psychiatrist to realize that Chris Reeve was probably one breath from suicide — literally. The man was struggling to simply breathe. I suspect to quit breathing would have been easy for him, and this was probably exactly what his doctors were worried about.

I have no idea how much money Chris had at the time of his accident but undoubtedly it was a lot. He was almost certainly a member of the "top two percent" economically in American society — probably in the top ten percent in the world. He was a white, still relatively young American, male, a movie star who was very successful. By most standards he had everything. Then he fell off his horse, and in an instant his life was transformed from that of the top two percent of American society to that of a quad, a young man with no use of his arms, hands, legs, hips. He could not walk, run, ski, ride. He could not turn on the TV with his hands, pick up a glass of beer, or have sex. His life had changed as much as a person's life can change in an instant. And for the worse.

Keeping a patient on the road to recovery in this situation is not an easy thing to do. I have a suspicion that his doctors, trying to make put positive spin on his situation to convince him to not simply quit breathing, said to him, "It could have been worse. You could have had a head injury."

And this of course was actually true. His condition could have been much worse with a TBI. But those were certainly not the words I needed to hear as I lay in bed in a rehabilitation hospital with a head injury.

I took what he said personally. And it hurt.

I hate to say it like this, but it's true: falling off The Grand Teton was every bit as traumatic for me as falling off a horse was for him. Poor Chris, and "but for the grace of god." It could have been me.

Chris died on October 10, 2004. May he rest in peace!

CHAPTER 9

I Choose Life. I Want to Live!

The first time I remember saying those words out loud was after I had moved to Boston. I had buried my mother a few years earlier, when I just turned 30. She was too young to die, and her death rolled around in my head for years. Much unfinished business.

Mom was from the WWII generation. It was a time when cigarette smoking was considered something to calm the nerves. The habit was socially accepted, even encouraged. Mom was addicted to nicotine, and by the time she was 50, her immune system was completely shot. It was only a matter of time until she got a bug that would bring her down. Mom was only 56 when she died!

I Choose Life

Being a young man in the Seventies in America was not easy, and my mother's death did not help the situation. I could not put it together. The whole youth thing; being an American; the good fight; cancer; women and relationships; having children; America in shambles; Nixon; Reagan; the cold war; the hostages; nuclear war and the end of life on earth; two minutes until midnight. It was all in there in my head. Everything was mixed up.

I did not figure any of it out. I simply left. A very good friend of mine was going to Boston to attend law school, and when she told me, I saw that as my escape. My ticket was civil rights, and I left.

What I left was a pretty good future. The place I worked was impressed with me and were prepared to send me to law school, for free if I would commit to work for them for 3 to 5 years after graduating. I liked doing civil rights work and this was a very good opportunity. But I was at crossroads. Something was wrong.

For years I'd been teaching classes in nonviolence and organizing marches, sit-ins and civil disobedience actions while others my age had been traveling to Europe and Asia. I had not gone anywhere and I'd never lived anywhere but the South. I sometimes felt I was on a permanent anthropology assignment. I thought that I didn't leave now, I would never leave. So, I left.

I ended up in a neighborhood in Boston called Allston, in a house where I was simply a rent check and I had to smoke my cigarettes out on the porch. I had a 20- by 25-foot room to myself, hardwood floors and a mattress on the floor. I found a beat up old TV that I got to working with an antenna made of wire and foil.

I'd sometimes reflect that I was living like either a monk or a college student, or both. When I was an organizer in Louisville, I had hundreds of friends. And the downside of having hundreds of friends is that hundreds of people know everything that has happened in your life. In Boston I had privacy. In many ways I did not even know why I needed it. But now, looking back, I see that I needed it because it gave me time to heal.

Allston had a surplus of used book stores, and in no time I was living in my room with 20 or so used books lying around. I had my mattress, the TV, my guitar, my typewriter and my bicycle, and that was my life. While living in this simple state, one day I said the words, "I want to live." Out loud. I remember saying them. It was the first time I had ever really reached the point of seeing things with such simple clarity: I could either continue the course I was on and die, or I could change and live.

I quit smoking within 6 months. I chose life. I wanted to live!

I have said those words more than once since that time.

Lying in bed at rehab watching *Downhill Racer* was one of those times. They were not hollow words.

Sometimes choices between life and death become simple. Lying in bed at the rehab hospital was one of those times. I chose life.

Over time, as my treatment continued, I began to see that much to my pleasant surprise, I was starting to "come back" more and more. Doctors were impressed. Things were looking up. I started talking more and understanding more. The downside of getting better, though, is that you begin realizing just how bad things are. Many of the questions we all had about my health and recuperation were still weeks, if not months to years away, and several of the biggest questions remained: Will I recover enough to ever get a job again? Will I recover enough to walk again? Drive? Hike? Ski? Bike? And then there was the huge question which everyone kind of avoided. What about sex?

The good news was that I was getting better, but no one knew how much better I would become.

CHAPTER 10

OJ — It Is Not About the Glove

Every morning when I woke up I would go through a 3- to 5-second period of disorientation. What is this institution? What is going on? Then I would start remembering that I was in a hospital, that I had been in a climbing accident, and so on. Part of every morning's wakeup was the sensation that something was wrong. Something was missing. Well, the "missing" part was the physical sensation that a part of me, a part of my brain, was missing; that all of Scott Houchin was not there. Remembering all this was an uphill struggle.

On this particular morning, besides everything else I was feeling, I was feeling that I had to go to the bathroom — and at that point in my rehab I was still not capable of walking. Thus, I needed to be assisted into a wheelchair. My pee bottle was not even half full, but that was only half the reason I needed to "hit the head" as they say.

So I pressed the call button for assistance and I turned on *Downhill Racer* to kill time. Usually it took a few minutes — sometimes longer in the morning, since all the patients needed to do the same thing I needed to do, and it was a brain injury ward and most of the patients were either in chairs or quads. You had to wait your turn.

Ten minutes went by. I pressed the button again. No one came. I called the nurse's station on my room phone — this was 1995 and we did not have cell phones. No answer.

Something was going on.

So I finally started the effort of getting myself into my wheelchair, which was no easy task. My left ankle was broken, and my right ankle was severely sprained (which was worse than broken in many ways). However, the hardest part was that my right arm was useless, and I am right-handed. My right wrist was badly broken in the fall and now I had an external fixator on it, which translates as "do not put any pressure on that arm." It was now a non-weight-bearing arm. I am in bed and my legs do not work and my primary arm, my right arm is useless. So when I say I needed someone to assist me in getting into the wheelchair, I am not joking.

But eventually, with great difficulty, I did succeed in loading myself into the wheelchair and went to the bathroom. Then I rolled out to the nurse's station to see what was going on.

No one there? This was a very odd situation! Almost always there was at least one person at the desk. Even in the middle of the night there was always at least one person on duty. That person was not allowed to leave the desk. They would call for help if needed, but they would never leave the desk unattended. At least that is what I thought. But there was no one there today.

Since I was in a wheelchair, I started exploring. With a walker it took me at least a full 2 minutes to go 100 feet. But in a chair, I could cover that distance in less than 15 seconds. I was mobile, and I began a lap around the rehab facility to find out what was going on. As I rounded a corner I ran into an employee assisting a patient who'd "had an accident," as they called it.

"Where are the nurses?" I asked her.

"In the TV room," she told me. "The OJ verdict is coming in."

It was October 3, 1995.

As I wheeled into the lobby, I saw them. Literally every employee — and most patients of the rehab facility — were sitting in the main lobby, which we called the TV room. They were glued to the television.

It was a mixed crowd: many of the doctors were Indian — Asian — or white; most of the nurses were white; most of the nursing assistants were either African-American or Hispanic. The custodial staff were mostly Hispanic or African American. In other words, it was your standard professional setup. The folks in charge were white. The professional workers were Asian or white and the assistants and floor workers African American or Hispanic. The patients in the room were also a mix. I had been a civil rights professional for over 15 years and I could pretty much do a racial breakdown with one glance. This group fit the typical American medical rehab hospital makeup.

All of them were milling around the television set in the lobby. Just like the rest of the country, everyone was watching to see what was going to happen.

I Choose Life

When the verdict came down, reaction in the room was split, just like the rest of the county. There were only a few African American patients but lots of African American employees, and although they were keeping their reactions low-key (probably to ensure they kept their jobs), you could tell that most of them were pleased.

But in the TV room that day, the whites outnumbered the African Americans at least 2 to 1. And the white people were visibly upset.

Because of my years of civil rights work, I thought I had a pretty good idea what was going on. I suspected the white people were getting a short but powerful jolt of something African Americans experienced frequently: seeing an obvious murderer walk when everybody with common sense knew that he did it.

I do not believe most African Americans believed that OJ was innocent. Quite the opposite. What I suspect was that most of them felt a kind of turning-the-tables satisfaction, knowing that white people had been murdering, raping, stealing, burning alive and lynching innocent African American people for hundreds of years with nobody (that is, white people) thinking much about it. I think they were just plain happy to see an African American male "getting away with it." For once, money and the system worked in favor of an African American man, instead of against him, which was almost always the case.

To white people, "justice" too often it means an African American man is going to be jailed, killed, burned alive, lynched, or beaten to death for some sort of crime against a white. That's justice in America, and I'm not thinking of just the 1800s. I have always been haunted by a photograph taken in Indiana, the state across the river from where I lived. In the photo a crowd of 40 or so white people, including children, are standing around with big smiles on their faces and two African American men are hanging from a tree. Dead! Lynched! This was not Mississippi. It was "the North" and it was 1930.

During my parents' lifetimes, and mine too for that matter, tens of thousands of African American men were put in jails and hundreds were routinely lynched, beaten to death and or burned alive for simply say-ing hello to a white woman or stealing a few dollars so their children could eat. Maybe they stole a car or sold some pot to a white guy. You name it: African Ameri-can men suffered for it. And it was the same for Afri-can American women. And African American people know this is what white people see as "justice".

I Choose Life

I think that for a lot African Americans the OJ trial simply felt to them like "justice."

For white people, though, the verdict said that a murdering animal had gone free simply because he could hire "good attorneys" and beat the rap. To their way of thinking, letting this African American man go free when he killed that beautiful white woman was unacceptable.

That is how I thought white people were viewing the OJ verdict.

As I wheeled myself back to my room, I instinctively felt all this. I'd spent over a decade investigating civil rights cases and reviewing cities and states all over the country for their civil rights performance, and I knew the sentiments and signs. I knew that within America civil rights issues were a flash point, that in a moment rational people could become enraged with anger. I have been in a room when a white person used the "n" word or called an African American male "a boy" and witnessed the spontaneous rage. Hundreds of years of terror and anger could boil to the surface in an instant with the simple mention of a word and the true horror of racism in America was exposed in the room. I have seen it firsthand. I knew this OJ verdict was just one incident in the ongoing

American saga regarding race.

I have also learned to keep my mouth shut when it comes to civil rights matters. The Civil War, the most destructive war in American history, was a horror worse than anything Hollywood will ever cook up on screen. The Civil War was fought over civil rights issues and really, it was not all that long ago.

So I went back to my room and got ready to go to PT. As I wheeled myself down the hall to the gym, I again said the words, "I want to live!"

CHAPTER 11

Going Home

When they started discussing the prospect of going home from the hospital, I was excited. I was really looking forward to going home.

Sharyn was concerned that if I went home, I wouldn't be getting all the therapies, testing, and recovery treatment I was getting at the hospital.

In my mind, "going home" was something much larger than going back to our apartment. To me, the phrase "going home" meant going back to my home before I had my accident. Throughout my treatment, due to my confusion from the injury, the term "home" meant going back to our apartment and the way I was before I had my accident. Of course, in this I was very much mistaken.

I could experience the actual brain injury itself; I could tell that something was wrong. It was almost like the sensation that there were two Scotts, the Scott before the accident and the Scott after the accident. At times I physically felt the difference in my mind, or at least I had the sensation that there was a difference.

Obviously, I wanted, intensely, to be the Scott that I was before the accident. I had a physical sensation that a part of me was missing and I wanted it back. In my confusion, being offered the chance to go home I took to be an offer to somehow go back to being the Scott before the accident. Of course I was very mistaken.

Sharyn fought to keep me in the hospital, but physically I started improving to the point where I could get around and take care of myself in terms of the usual life-skill chores, and the testing proved it. So they sent me home.

"Home" was not returning to being the Scott before the accident. Mostly it was just hours of being alone. At least I got to hang with my bro, Cougar our cat. I did all my exercises every day, both physical and mental exercises. Every day. Several times a day. Day after

59

day. Week after week.

Weeks turned into months. I was getting bored, but I was also getting better. Eventually it became time to see if I could ever return to work.

CHAPTER 12

Work

When I was injured, my job was with the Federal Government. There were several disability employment laws that would protect me. So, unless I could not perform "the essential functions of the job," I would remain employed.

I had taken my job very seriously before my accident. I had basically become a wizard when it came to reading and comprehending the thousands of words of the CFR — the Code of Federal Regulations. The federal agency I worked for distributed tens of millions of dollars a day, and proposals of this kind to spend a significant amount of those dollars came across my desk for review. The ability to interpret federal regulations when large amounts of money are involved is a good skill to have.

After I returned to work — part-time at first — I would go down to our law library during lunch and read case law to help bring back my vocabulary and my ability to follow sequence and logic. There is usually a simple logic to most precedent-setting cases. Reading the cases helped to bring Scott back.

After a very short time back on the job, I had re-familiarized myself with the regulations and I was again "the wizard". I was safe. I returned to my job full-time.

TBI survivors have a number of "cuts" they either make — or don't make — as they recover. First, they must make the cut of going home from rehab. Some make that cut; others never do.

Being allowed to drive a car was a big cut. Some made the cut; others didn't.

Returning to work was also a very big cut. It surprised me how many TBI folks I met in group therapy that had never made that cut. They had lost their jobs and could not find another one. Most, I suspected, had lost their jobs in violation of employment antidiscrimination laws. Employers are supposed to attempt to "reasonably accommodate" disabled employees.

But as I listened to my TBI colleagues talking about their former jobs and how they'd lost them, I could tell from what they were saying that they'd almost certainly been treated illegally; that is, they'd lost their job due to illegal discrimination based upon disability. However, I also knew that if they did not have a lawyer and/or $50,000 to sue in state or federal court, their chances of getting their jobs back were minimal.

I was fortunate. I made all the cuts. I made the cut to leave the institution. I made the cut to drive my car. Finally, I made the cut to keep my job. I was on my way back to my life before the accident.

Standing on top of the Grand Teton.

Starting to come out of "the cloud".

Scott – the train wreck. Note the external fixator on my right arm.

I Choose Life

My Bro Cougar.

With my friend Ken.

Staring down the Black Ice Couloir.

CHAPTER 13

DIG

Once I felt my competence and output at work had returned to my pre-injury level, I started looking for ways to improve the rights of the disabled workers in my agency. I worked with other disabled civil rights advocates daily. We sat close to each other, and before long we had formed a group. We called ourselves DIG, for Disabled In Government. When our numbers increase to 10, we started having regular meetings to plan what we wanted to do. One of our most important and successful campaigns was to insure accessible parking for all employees and clients of our agency.

You'd think an agency that enforced civil rights laws would want to be in compliance with the very laws there were enforcing. But this was not always the case. I never saw it as an act of malice; it seemed simply that the agency got so busy with other issues that they never got around to complying themselves. It was a time when federal agency budgets were being cut. We were expected to do as much work as always but with less money and staff. All these factors may have explained why we weren't complying with disability laws, but we in DIG felt that nonetheless our agency had to become more aware of its responsibilities.

DIG was fortunate in that, when we were the most active, the regional administrator of our agency was a very progressive person who himself had a disability. He supported our efforts to get accessible parking for the agency. When it happened, he sent out an e-mail stating how proud he was that there were new disability parking spaces in our garage, and he congratulated DIG on its success.

He also helped DIG get good reasonable accommodation policies established.

Soon we were starting DIG chapters in federal agencies around the country. It was great to see disabled federal employees working together on disability rights. We became more aggressive and started a series of "lunch and learn" sessions on disability issues.

I Choose Life

I discovered that if you want to get a crowd of federal employees to attend a presentation, offer a free lunch and "they will come"!

It works!

DIG started doing various lunch and learns on all the disability issues you can think of. We went through just about all the disability organizations in town and then we started having the disability law firms come and speak. After that, I started expanding my search and it turns out that one of my heroes from the days of *Downhill Racer*, Jimmy Heuga is also a disability activist. I mentioned Jimmy earlier when discussing the "Innsbruck Era" and American men winning our first alpine medals ever. Well Jimmy was one of the two Americans winning our first medals. However, Jimmy also developed multiple sclerosis (MS) shortly after winning his medal.

Back in those days when Jimmy first started having to deal with the symptoms of MS, America was not really all that aware of the disease. Jimmy became a very popular advocate/spokesperson for MS and he only lived about 30 miles from Denver in Louisville, Colorado. So, I called him up to see if he would like to speak to our group. I explained that I'd been a big fan since childhood and I then invited him to come to

Denver and speak to our group. I said that he would be quite an inspiration to DIG folks and the folks in my agency since many of them were skiers and had known about him for decades. Further, I told him I could guarantee a full house.

This was in 2006 and I could tell just from talking to him that he was having a hard time with his MS. Apparently, the symptoms were getting worse and his health status was deteriorating due to the disease. Jimmy explained that he could not do speaking engagements due to the disease. He said he was sorry because it sounded like the sort of audience he liked to speak to. However, he was going to have to decline the invitation.

Jimmy Heuga died on February 8, 2010 and the State of Colorado, along with the rest of the ski community in America, mourned his death.

I continued looking for another speaker and I remembered another "star" from the Innsbruck Era who could possibly be a speaker. Jill Kinmont was an Olympic hopeful skier for the USA and she made the cover of *Sports Illustrated*, which was no small accomplishment for a women skier back in those days. Part of the publicity surrounding Jill focused on the relationship between her and Buddy Werner, another of the Innsbruck Era men's hopefuls. On one of Jill's runs down the hill she had a bad accident and was paralyzed, permanently, losing the use of her lower body.

I knew about Jill due to a movie that came out about her struggle in 1975 called *The Other Side of the Mountain*. The movie was the story of her accident and her struggle back from the paralyzing accident. The film was a very popular back in the 1970s and it swept the country. Her story and the movie were a big success and a very inspirational story for public regarding disability issues.

I called her up.

She was touched that I had called, but Jill was about 70 years old when I called and she had not been doing any public speaking in a long time. As with Jimmy, her health was fragile at that point and she could not travel.

Jill died a few years later in 2012.

DIG continued with the Lunch and Learn series, though, and soon we were starting DIG chapters in federal agencies around the country. It was great to see disabled federal employees working together on disability rights.

I retired from the federal government in 2008, and probably the biggest thing I missed, besides the paycheck, was working with fellow disabled employees.

CHAPTER 14

Brain Injury Meetings

At first, I was hesitant to attend Brain Injury Association meetings, because of what might get back to my employer.

In my job as a civil rights professional, I'd seen how destructive an employer can be when a disabled employee files a complaint. I'd seen firsthand how casual information about an employee can be used by an employer to fight the complaint. It is not a nice thing to see happening.

Here's how such casual information often gets back to an employee: Fellow employees visit their hurt colleague in the hospital, then the well-meaning colleagues talk about the patient at work, never realizing they are providing information/evidence for the employer to use against the employee. It reminded me of what happened in the "Prague Spring": young activists took photos of the Soviet invasion, and the photos included the demonstrators fighting the invasion. Little did the photographers realize the Soviets would take their cameras, develop the film, then round up the demonstrators in the photos. Photographers hoping to show the world the injustice they were witnessing were instead giving the occupiers evidence to use against the demonstrators.

A few comments made nonchalantly back at work by well-wishers could sabotage my efforts to come back to my old job. If colleagues came to visit and I could not remember their names — after working with them for years — that would be noticed, and not in a good way. And if this was then discussed at work by my colleagues where others would hear it. That is what I worried about. A few comments like that and an employer can start building a case against the employee, using the employee's friends as witnesses.

This is not paranoia. It has happened many times. Employers do not want employees that appear to be "slow" or less productive, and as a generalization, most people incorrectly (and illegally) assume that someone with a head injury who has difficulty remembering names is "slow". It makes no difference that these sorts of discriminatory stereotypes are not true and that basing employment decisions on them is illegal: after all, that is what illegal discrimination is all about. I had seen this sort of thing happen too many times. It is unfortunate that our world is like that, but I knew what could happen.

The one exception to the rule of no visitors was my longtime friend Ken. We had been friends for decades. Ken was a professional banjo player and I was a wannabee guitar player and we have been good friends since we met playing music.

When my accident happened, Ken was a good support person. Not only did he offer constant moral support, but he literally came to our rescue. When I was in the hospital in Idaho, Sharyn was spending all her time taking care of me. But someone had to drive the car we drove to the Tetons back to Denver. Ken stepped up to the job — no questions asked. He did that, and numerous other chores — no questions asked. He has always been there when we needed him. Ken always has been and continues to be a very good friend.

§

So of course there was worry about me participating in group meetings of the Brain Injury Association. In an employment discrimination case (if I had to sue to get my job back), the folks at a group meeting like this could be called as witnesses or provide evidence against me. We did not know the people in the Brain Injury Association, or what they would say if there was a lawsuit.

Eventually, though, I decided to go the meetings anyway. It was a very good decision. Being in a room full of other TBI survivors was just what the doctor ordered. Finally I was with people who understood exactly what I was going through.

One of the first things we did every meeting was put on name tags. Even after several months of meeting on a regular basis, even though we all recognized each other's faces and had shared incredibly private intimate information with each other, we could not remember each other's names.

You can imagine what we shared: hygiene issues, sex issues, how to handle our doctors, how to handle our spouses, how to handle our insurance companies, what medications worked and what didn't. A lot of very sensitive info. But we could not remember each other's names. It was short-term memory loss.

It was such a comfort to be in a room where no-body expected you to remember their name.

Not remembering names is a symptom of a TBI. We lose the ability for short-term memory or word recall. Someone we have known for years walks up, and for about 10 seconds our brains will not be able to pull up the person's name. We recognize their face, and remember our friendship; not remembering the name is simply a sign of a TBI. Unfortunately, outside of TBI meetings, people do not understand this and frequently it causes problems. People are offended when you do not remember their name. I could write books on this. In fact, doctors and therapist do write books on this.

The Brain Injury Association group sessions were the first time I could openly talk about how to deal with doctors. It turns out that almost all of us were having trouble communicating with our doctors. This does not mean that doctors were not sympathetic to us and did not treat us well. It was just that they had not experienced the symptoms, therefore, it was hard for them to understand what was really going on. We pretty much all agreed that doctors did not get it. The simplest way to describe it is to say that doctors listen to you, but they have pretty much already made up their mind what is going on regardless of what you say. They frequently heard our words and then reassured us that "That will pass and get better," when actually it was getting worse. Headaches were a good example. An even better example was the feeling of being detached from ourselves. Many of us had the feeling that we simply were "not all there". Part of us, our being, felt like it had been lost in the TBI and in all of our therapies we were simply trying to get back to where we were prior to our accident. It was almost a physical sensation that we were missing a part of our self.

We all needed to talk about sex, and in our group was the only safe place to do that. After a TBI, sex is pretty much impossible, at least for a while. Some of us were coming around after a few months but then others were not, and some had basically lost all interest in sex. What started out as a very hush sort of embarrassing part of our group discussions became a very important part of our meetings. Most of us had a girlfriend, wife, boyfriend, husband or some sort of significant other, and we were very concerned that our mate was going to leave us. Our sex life became an issue, as well as what we needed to do to keep our mate. Having your wife or husband divorce you after a TBI was not all that unusual; talking openly with your mate about sex or not wanting to have sex was about the last thing you wanted to do. Our routine meetings became the one place where we could openly and honestly talk to each other about what was going on with us and what we feared.

No one had to explain to us how bad it would be if we lost our girlfriend, wife, boyfriend, or husband. More than one person had come to the group and described how a significant other had decided they just could not go on with the relationship due to the TBI because the survivor "had changed." It was routinely discussed that we had changed somewhat, but the reality is that most of us had changed significantly and the thought we were going to lose our companion scared us to death.

In some ways, we felt like "our group" was our new family.

CHAPTER 15

Getting Back On The Horse — Or In This Case, The Bike

It was a long climb back onto a bike. For the first six months after my fall, the big question was: would I ever be able to walk like I used to? The next big hurdle was: will I be able to walk and hike like I used to? The answer to that one was "no." After my accident I could not hike at all without poles. I used them for balance.

The big question after that was: will I ever be able to climb again:? Sharon answered that one for me. "It's me or climbing,' she said. "Choose."

I chose her, and a wise decision it was.

About returning to climbing: After my fall I really

didn't even want to return to climbing. I had noticed a disturbing pattern among climbers. When someone had a tragic climbing accident, we, the still-active climbers, would start doing a 1,2,3 analysis of the fallen climber's mistakes, and what mistakes we would not make, rationalizing to ourselves that it was safe for us to keep climbing. In reality it was simply a form of denial. Like I said, "There are bold climbers and there are old climbers but there are no old, bold climbers."

Physically, I was used up. My sense of balance was permanently damaged. I worked very hard in PT to regain my sense of balance and eventually I got from a "2" to a "6", with "1" being that I did not have the balance to stand up and "10" being that I had regained the same balance I had prior to the accident.

I have not really progressed past a 6 – 7ish level. I will never have the balance to put my full weight on the front points of a crampon while on vertical ice. I simply do not have the balance. Still, 20 years later, I cannot hike without using my poles.

About the bike: The big question was, "Will I ever be able to ride a bike again?" The answer was "yes."

Prior to learning how to climb, my number-one sport was bicycling. I did it as much as I climbed. "I loved it" is the simplest way to describe it. When I moved to New England and learned how to climb, I put my bicycle away. After my accident, I decided to ride again, but I could not ride a bike. I recognized this almost immediately. I did try to ride a bit and realized that I would hurt myself if I tried to ride. I simply had no sense of balance. Back to PT.

Endless hours of standing in a doorjamb on one foot and then bending my knee as far down as I could and then straightening it back up. A set of 10, then rest. Then a set of 25. Rest. A set of 50 and then the other leg. The same drill. At least three times a day. Day after day. Week after week. Then when I got good at that I did it with my eyes closed. The same drill. Day after day. Week after week.

My PT/OT called it "rewiring the brain for balance". Eventually, over a very long time, it worked. I got better. Over the course of a couple of years, I got even better. I regained enough balance to hike moderate hills. Then at Year Three I attempted a bicycle. It worked.

I had found my new sport. A better way to say this is that I re-discovered bicycling. It became one of my passions. When I ride I feel like a kid again!

I got better on the bike. I started doing metric centuries — 100-kilometer bike rides — as often as

83

possible. Back in the Seventies when Colorado started a lottery, a portion of the profits by law went to the building of bike paths, and now Denver has literally hundreds of miles of bike paths. I signed up for some bike tours. There are many charity bike tours in Colorado. I started signing up for them and discovered that I was capable of completing them and they were fun. I loved it.

Riding on charity bike tours with many riders also means that you see riders get hurt. Several times I witnessed serious bike accidents. One made a difference in my life. We were riding down Tennessee Pass outside Leadville, Colorado, going towards Minturn when a woman went down. She was badly hurt: unconscious and bleeding in several places. Many of the folks standing around her were medical professionals, but they had no experience in emergency medicine on a road in the middle of nowhere. We had no cell coverage either, so several of us had to ride miles down the road to get cell coverage just in order to call 911. I later learned she had survived, but I realized that bicyclists need medics on their rides — medical professionals trained in how to keep the patient alive until the ambulance gets there.

That experience had a permanent effect on me. I became interested in learning how to treat injured bike riders. Turns out, people who treat injuries "in the field", so to speak, are called emergency medical technicians (EMTs).

I'd gotten back on the bike and was hooked. Now I had to get the EMT thing done.

CHAPTER *16*

"If You Drop the Baby Pick It Up"
EMT School

I was grandpa. Most of my fellow students were kids in their early 20s or younger. I was in my late 50s. When I enrolled in EMT school, I didn't realize that becoming an EMT was a new route to becoming a doctor. But apparently if you are 22 and you do not get into medical school right out of college, Plan B is to go to EMT school and do emergency medicine for a couple of years, then work your way into medical school from the inside. Get a job in an emergency room and get to know the right people. Obtain lots of good experience, then suck up to the right people, and you find yourself accepted into medical school.

This was the plan for several of my classmates. They were B-plus to A-minus students in pre-med undergraduate programs. Smart kids. And here I was in a class with them. Me, TBI and all.

I also didn't know EMT school would be run para-military fashion. We were assigned large reading assignments in medical books, every night. Our EMT book was about 1,400 pages long — with small print — with several facts per page you had to memorize in order to pass the course. We were tested every other day. If you did not maintain an 80 percent average you flunked. It was sink or swim! I swam, but about a third of my class sank.

Here I was, over 50, survivor of a traumatic brain injury and suffering from serious short-term memory loss, competing with kids right out of college with GPAs of over 3.0. No sweat!

I learned that I loved patient care. All those years as a federal employee involved in doing civil rights, I had been dealing constantly with conflict between humans. Allegations, sworn statements, depositions, fighting over money, class warfare, fighting over race, fighting for a safe place to live, fighting for a safe place to raise your kids, and fighting for a good place for your kids to go to school so that they would not have to live in the neighborhood where you grew up. It was a fight for the middle class, and the key ingredients were hate, fear, greed and prejudice. I was the investigator who talked to the people on all sides. There was nothing but walls on all sides. The only human contact was conflict. I desperately missed real, kind human contact.

Patient care is the exact opposite. When people are badly hurt, they want help. If you know how to help them, then you are welcomed. You are the good guy. The more hurt they are, the more they want you to help them.

I found I had missed this kind of human contact.

Even more important, when people are hurt there is no bullshit. No one is trying to convince me of anything. No one is trying to lie their way out of something. When people are hurt there is no pretense. The work is simply about dealing with the patient, their pain, and keeping them alive. There are no arguments, only treatment. It is close human contact at its best. I love patient care!

For six months I did nothing but go to class, study, take tests, eat and sleep. I had a ski pass good for resorts all over Colorado but I didn't go skiing once that winter. I didn't have time. EMT School was very hard work.

About "dropping the baby": One morning an instructor used this phrase as he described how to assist a mother in delivering a baby. It was not a tongue-in-cheek comment. When babies push out of the mother. They are extremely slippery, we learned, and the EMT should be prepared, because it is difficult to hold the baby along with the 50 other things we are having to remember to do as the baby crowns and pushes out. I personally like the comment because it captures and crystallizes the entire attitude of being an EMT. What most people think of as the unthinkable we have to deal with in a very matter of fact, simple manner. So "If you drop the baby — pick it up!"

CHAPTER 17

Ski Patrol

Even though I was now an EMT, I was hesitant to start signing up for rides as a bike medic. So I started out by doing ski patrol. Good decision! I quickly determined that I was much better in the First Aid Room (FAR) room than I was a skier, and in the FAR I saw many more patients. The more patients I saw the more I liked being an EMT/Ski patroller.

Ski injuries are similar to bicycle injuries: a large number of broken wrists, broken collarbones, dislocated shoulders, head injuries and bloody injuries — and since it is Colorado, a lot of altitude sickness and dehydration issues. Most of the time, either a skier had wrecked and was hurt, or someone had run into the skier. Sometimes skiers hit trees or ski equipment on the hill.

Frequently my job was simply to immobilize the skier's injuries, keep the patient stabilized and prepare them for transport to a hospital.

There were a wide variety of injuries, and I liked treating them.

On my 60th birthday I treated one of my most interesting cases. It was a cardiac incident and I was first on the scene. I had to make all the decisions, including calling for advanced life support.

It was a very cold and sunny day at the Colorado ski resort where I was patrolling. The previous day had been the slowest day of the year in the FAR — not a single patient all day. This day looked to be turning out pretty much the same. Only one patient had required any real attention all morning.

At midday I'd gone up the hill to the top patrol hut where they were serving very good cheeseburgers. I had a great lunch as I looked out at the surrounding snow-capped Rocky Mountains. I ate my fill and relaxed a bit. Then it was back to the bottom of the hill and the FAR.

When I arrived, I relieved the patroller on duty

and told her to go get some lunch, as is standard procedure. I was still relaxing after a good meal. I made some coffee to stay awake. If anything came up, I figured I'd send for reinforcements.

A woman came in and said that her husband was having trouble breathing and asked if I could help her. I grabbed the radio, my pack of medical supplies, and we were off. From her description of his location I thought he was in the Lodge, but she took me outside where he was lying on the snow. When she had left him a few minutes ago he was standing, but now he was lying on the snow and a crowd was forming around him. I went over to treat my patient.

"I'm having trouble breathing, my chest hurts and so does my back," he said.

"How long ago did this start?" I asked him. "About 20 minutes ago. It hurts more now than it did a minute ago," he said.

You do not have to go to medical school to recognize that this description sounds a great deal like a significant cardiac event. These were the typical signs of a myocardial infarction — that is, a heart attack.

My training kicked in: I could determine just how "sick" the patient was later but first I had to summon help. I pulled my radio out and called for a "trauma pack," with oxygen and an automated external defibrillator, or AED, more patrollers, and a sled. Then I focused on the most important call that the first on-site patroller must make: telling dispatch to call 911 and to have the responders run "urgent" (with lights and sirens) — and to tell then that this was a possible Flight for Life evacuation. "Over and out," said Dispatch. And the cavalry — my colleague patrollers — were on their way.

Back to my patient.

I pulled out my notepad and began to eliminate all the other possibilities. I questioned his family: "Does he have a history of diabetes?" "History of epilepsy? Allergies? History of asthma?" These were the sorts of illnesses that might cause difficulty breathing, fainting, and altered mental status. My questioning was over in 20 seconds. I saved "cardiac issues" for last. I knew this was probably the correct diagnosis, and I wanted to eliminate all the others first.

According to his wife, the patient had no history of cardiac events. He did take high blood pressure medication, she said, but he had never had any heart trouble. So he had no nitroglycerin pills or other medications to relieve a heart attack.

93

I Choose Life

I pulled out my scissors and began cutting away anything I could see that might restrict his breathing as I asked his family a few more questions. Unfortunately, they were "flatlanders" from the East Coast who had just come to Colorado for a ski trip, and so they weren't used to the altitude. Altitude is always more of a factor than almost anyone gives it credit for.

All the elements were there to cause a cardiac event: hard exercise, being at a higher altitude than normal, and being middle aged. I really wished I had some oxygen to give him.

A few seconds later I saw the cavalry coming to our rescue just like something from a John Wayne movie. A half-dozen "red coats and white crosses" — the ski patrollers had arrived! The lead red coat had a cylinder of oxygen with a non-re-breather mask attached. O2 — oxygen — is probably the best intervention for a medical situation like this. I immediately started breathing myself; I realized I'd been acting on pure adrenaline till now. As the lead patroller attached the oxygen mask, I whispered in the ear of the patient that he would now find it easier to breathe.

As usual, the oxygen worked, and less than a minute later he told me he felt a little better. But he was not even close to being out of the woods. A head-to-

toe examination and check of his vital signs revealed a weak and thready pulse, and he was soaked in sweat — all classic signs of a heart attack. I consulted with a senior patroller, and we loaded the patient onto a sled to take him to the FAR.

We continued administering oxygen. We got the AED ready and prepared the patient in case we had to perform CPR and use the AED. His vital signs remained constant, but he was fading in and out of consciousness. Finally the ambulance arrived, with all the "life pack" technology of modern American medicine: an EKG machine, pulse/oxygen monitor, an IV and fluids. The paramedic gave the patient some aspirin as I prepped him on patient's condition and history and told him what interventions we'd done.

The paramedic team took over. They'd contacted "Flight for Life." The man was going be airlifted by helicopter to Denver and some of the best cardiac treatment available. I explained this to the wife. As I spoke to her, it seemed that she now understood what all of us believed — this patent was now out of the woods. He was going to make it.

The ambulance took off for the hospital with running lights and sirens. Flight for Life was waiting at the hospital to take the patient to Denver.

I Choose Life

Two hours later we got the call from a paramedic in the ambulance crew: The patient was at a hospital and in a stable medical condition. They were running test to find out what exactly was going on with the heart rhythms. "So he made it?" I asked?

"Oh, yeah. He made it," the paramedic replied. "You guys did a good job." That was about as great a birthday present a new EMT/Ski Patroller could ever get.

I've now treated hundreds of patients in FARs all over Colorado, but none has had such an impact on me.

Although this still ranks as one of the most dramatic events I have had on a ski hill, I have treated a lot of other incidents. It seems the worst events happen at the end of the shift. One night at a "Night Skiing" resort, a snow boarder fell and broke his femur on the last run of the night. In the EMT world broken femurs are not a small item. If the break is mid-shaft the patient can easily go into shock, and to make matters worse, the large muscles of the thigh usually spasm, which can cause the broken bones to cut and tear tissue around the injury. The principal worry is injury to the femoral artery, which is one of the largest arteries in the body.

Treating a mid-shaft broken femur requires a tremendous amount of immediate concentrated medical care. Frequently it is necessary to put traction on the leg while still out on the hill. A patient can easily die from a mid-shaft broken femur.

Fortunately, a broken femur is not always a mid-shaft break. This snowboarder broke his femur where it attaches to the pelvic bone, so we did not have to put him in traction. However, he broke it just as we were closing the hill for the night. We still had to do sweep of the hill to be sure no one was still out on the hill, injured; we had to treat him, and we had to close the FAR for the night. It was the graveyard shift. But we got it all done.

When we put the snowboarder on the sled to transport him off the hill, we realized we needed a pad under is knee to stabilize it. We were already using all the blankets we had to keep him warm (a patient in shock and cold weather is not a good mix). Since we didn't have anything, I took off my pack and used it as a support pillow. The resort was closing for the night, and as the ambulance drove off with the patient to the hospital, I realized my pack was still under his knee. They wouldn't be bringing my pack back to me that night. It was possible that in their haste to treat the patient my pack might just be thrown to the side, and thrown out when they cleaned the ER.

My wallet was in that pack! I needed it back.

So that night after the resort closed I had to drive all the way to the hospital on ice-packed roads. When I got to the ER they were considering surgery on the patient and, to be honest, the last thing they cared about was my pack. I did receive several compliments about our prompt and accurate treatment of the patient, but as it ended up I did not retrieve my pack with my wallet until the wee hours of the morning. Getting it back required sitting around waiting for hours.

The patient with the broken femur — a kid in his twenties — was sent to Denver for surgery. He would probably heal and go "wreck himself" in the terrain park again. I was told the prognosis was very good for that guy.

The injury that worries me that most while doing ski patrol is head injury. A skier's head can hit the snow in a fall, or a tree in a crash. There can be a head-on collision with another skier. When the head hits an object, sometimes veins or arteries are ruptured. When it's a vein, it's called a "subdural" hematoma; when it is an artery, it's an 'epidural" hematoma. The blood from the ruptured vein/artery has nowhere to go. The skull has a finite amount of space and the brain fills most of it. When the pooling blood (hematoma) increases, it pushes the brain out of the way. Combined with the brain swelling due to the accident, this can cause extreme pressure within the skull, which means damage to the brain tissue. If not caught in time it can easily mean death. Time is tissue.

When veins are ruptured, the bleeding is usually slow, and it may take a few days before symptoms of brain injury start appearing. Unfortunately, in too many cases, when symptoms appear it is already too late. When an artery is ruptured the bleeding's much faster. Still, by the time symptoms start appearing it may be too late to prevent permanent brain damage.

Probably the most famous case of something like this happening involved Natasha Richardson, wife of film actor Liam Neeson. According to the newspapers Natasha fell on a "bunny slope" in Quebec and went to the Ski Patrol First Aid Hut where she was seen by patrollers. The patrollers recommended that she go to a hospital to see if she had a subdural or epidural hematoma. Natasha elected not to go to the hospital, though, and returned to her room at the inn. Later that night, when she complained of a headache, the hotel contacted the paramedics who again advised her to go to the hospital, but again she decided not to. The next morning her condition was significantly worse.

I Choose Life

She died from an epidural hematoma.

An event like this is every ski patroller's nightmare: a patient who declines treatment then later dies from the injury. These sorts of injuries are very treatable if caught in time. The best way to determine the amount of injury is from a CT scan or MRI. Again, time is tissue.

It's natural that I am sensitive to head injuries. Whenever I treat a patient in a situation where a sub/epidural hematoma is possible. I do everything I can to convince them to get an MRI or CT scan. When I work in the FAR or as a medic on bike rides, I constantly worry about patients sustaining a subdural or epidural hematoma.

CHAPTER 18

Bike Medic

After a few years as a ski patroller, I got the confidence to become a riding medic on bicycle rides. There are an abundance of charity benefit bike rides in Colorado and all of them utilize riding medics. From non-bike riders I always hear, "Why have a medic if they are 10 miles behind the injured bicyclist and it will take an hour for them to reach the patient?" But the bicycling community in Colorado has come to realize this is rarely an issue. Almost always when a bicyclist goes down, a medic will appear within a few minutes. It's not really clear why this is, but it has proven to be true on hundreds of rides all over Colorado.

Most of the time there's 1 medic for every 50 riders.

I Choose Life

On some bigger rides the ratio is 1 to 25. Even though it's not planned, the bike medics eventually end up spread out fairly evenly along a bike course. When we medics realize we're bunching up, we spread out. No one has to say anything. It is just common sense. It works!

When an accident happens, our primary job is to keep the patient alive and as comfortable as possible until the ambulance arrives, following the correct medical protocols on the patient handoff to the ambulance team. This may sound simple, and in many cases, it is. But one of my first cases as a bike medic was the exception.

It was the "Ride the Rockies" bike ride, and the year was the 2011. I was one of about 30 medics under our medical director, "Doctor John". The "Ride the Rockies" bike ride is one of the most famous in America. People drive and fly in from all over the country to participate in this ride. It's usually six days long and covers 400 to 550 miles. Hearing this, most people think "hard ride!" But the distance is not the hard part. Covering up to 100 miles a day for six days in a row is reasonably hard on flat ground, but any bicyclist that takes the proper training can pull that off.

But "Ride the Rockies" is riding for six days and

covering 500 miles or so at elevations of 20,000 to 30,000 feet. That's a higher "elevation gain" than climbing Mt. Everest! Riders are not only covering nearly 100 miles but ascending 3,000 to 5,000 feet each day — for six days in a row. It is not the hardest ride in Colorado, but it is a ride that has a significant amount of prestige associated with it.

The ride is in June. In 2011, I spent the entire month of May training for it. Day after day. Rain or shine, training for RTR.

Every year is a different route. That year, there were 2,000 of us starting in Crested Butte and ending up in Georgetown. We'd cover approximately 414 miles with an elevation gain of a little over 23,000 feet. We had three monster passes to go over: Cottonwood Pass; Rabbit Ears Pass; and Berthoud Pass. Cottonwood Pass is the highest pass in Colorado at over 12,000 feet. It's between Crested Butte and Buena Vista. Rabbit Ears pass is just outside Steamboat going toward Kremmling. Berthoud Pass is on the route from Winter Park to Empire. All these passes are hard.

I spent the first night in the gym at Crested Butte. The options for overnights are: camp, stay in the gym, or find your own housing. I could write books on why it is best to stay in the gym. However, I will simply say that going to the bathroom in the middle of the night is about ten times easier if you are staying in the gym rather than camping in a tent. Plus, the gym is a flush toilet, and the first rule of bicycle touring is "never pass up a flush toilet".

I stayed in the gym. After morning coffee, I started riding. It was a cold morning. Probably only in the mid-40s, and we were riding downhill for the first 15 miles or so. I put on every piece of bike clothing I had, and it was still a very cold ride down to Almont at 8 in the morning. We made the turn off to Cottonwood Pass and started climbing. I believe Cottonwood is an altitude gain of somewhere between 3,500 and 4,000 feet. It was probably only 9 in the morning, but it already felt like a long day.

I treated my first patient at about 11,500 feet. A guy about my age had taken a fall. He had a serious cut on his right knee. I pulled over and started doing all the basics and treating the wound. He was going to need stitches — probably more than 10 of them, I thought. Lots of blood. I was applying direct pressure to stop the bleeding when another medic, Harry Jos, showed up and helped me out. Harry was a policeman from New York City and this was his first RTR.

We patched up the patient, then Harry took off and

I was left to finish up and do the paperwork, since I was first on scene. I started riding again three or four minutes after Harry left. We were only another quarter mile up the road when Harry yelled at me, "Hurry up, Scott! We have another patient!" I put the pedal to the metal — at least as much as I could at almost 12,000 feet.

When I got to the patient, I found a serious situation. The patient, a male about my age, had been riding a tandem bike with his 13-year-old daughter when he just fell off. Now he was lying unconscious on the ground. According to the daughter, it had just happened a few minutes earlier.

Both Harry and I realized the patient was not breathing; he was in cardiac arrest. I'd been teaching CPR for the Red Cross for a number of years, and now all that time as a CPR instructor paid off. Big time.

As first on scene, Harry was the lead medic, and he took control. He'd check the patient for life signs. He ordered me to try to find support. An ambulance.

There was no cell phone reception, so took off back down the hill looking for someone with a radio. I'd gone about 30 yards when I saw a Wheatridge Cyclery truck coming up the road. I knew they would have a radio. I flagged them down.

"Do you have a radio?"

"Yes" said the driver, "but only for emergency use."

"We have an emergency. I'm a medic. We have a patient who's having a heart attack. We need an ambulance. Immediately!"

I asked if they were in contact with the medical cars.

"They should hear the radio call," he said.

"Tell them we have a probable cardiac incident and that we need O2 and an AED. Please get a medical car up to 11,500 feet on the way up Cottonwood Pass. We have an unresponsive male approximately 50 years of age."

I left the driver to get the word out and returned to the patient, who was doing agonal breathing — that is, he was gasping for breath, which is not real breathing. He had no pulse. I told Harry I was a CPR instructor and that we needed to do CPR, with someone doing the breaths and someone doing compressions. Harry got his pocket mask (a light weight plastic device that helps with doing breaths into a patient), and started. Another medic who'd arrived started doing compressions. I kept saying, "The ratio is 30 compressions and then 2 breaths, 30 compressions and 2 breaths."

While the other medic was doing compressions, I ripped the biker's shirt off to "get to skin". "Count off the number of compressions out loud," I told them. We needed to monitor for both the accurate timing of compressions and the depth of compressions.

The medic doing compressions was experienced, but he was starting to get tired after a couple of rounds of compressions and breaths, so I took over compressions and Harry did the breaths. About this time the medical car showed up with the much-needed AED. When it was attached it showed we needed to shock the patient. First shock, and the patient still did not have a pulse. I told the medics to do what the AED told them to do, and another medic jumped in to do compressions. We continued with the cycle of compressions and breaths until the AED signaled it was time for another shock. Second shock and still no pulse.

I went looking for the patient's daughter. I found her about 100 feet up the road. Fortunately, a smart woman had led her away from the scene and as I walked up, the teen asked, "How is Dad doing?" I realized she had no idea how serious the situation was. By now her dad had been on the ground with compressions going on for over ten minutes; he had already been given two shocks with the AED and had showed no response. It did not look good — it did not look good at all. So I simply told her what medical people have been telling families for centuries. "We are doing all we can," I said.

Out of the daughter's hearing range, I informed the woman who'd been shepherding the girl that things did not look good, and asked her to try to keep the daughter away from where we were working on her dad.

I walked back, fully expecting to hear that a third and fourth shock had also been unsuccessful, but just then a surprised medic said, "We got a pulse!" Sure enough, I looked down at the pulse oximeter I'd put on man's finger at the start of the incident and saw he indeed had a pulse. Another medic, checking patient's carotid artery, said he was also now getting a faint pulse.

The ambulance showed up and what those ambulance medics can do is simply amazing. We volunteer medics now took a back seat to the ambulance crew with their equipment and skill. The patient lived. He was taken by Flight for Life to Denver and is walking around today.

During the half hour we worked on the patient at the side of the road, a couple hundred bicyclists rode by. That night in Buena Vista, word had gotten out to the couple of thousand bicyclists there that earlier in the day one of their fellow riders had down with a heart attack and had been saved by the bike medics. I was recognized as one of the medics who'd worked to save the patient, and again like something out of the movies, I did not have to buy a beer all night. In fact, I had to start turning down free beers because after three of them I realized I was going be very hung over for the ride the next day.

It was the only time I can ever remember when I was considered a hero. But of course, being at the right place at the right time had more to do with being a hero than anything else.

I was teaching CPR for the Red Cross back in those days, and when the Red Cross found out about the RTR incident they gave all of us — Harry, the other medics and me — the "Red Cross Lifesaver Award," the highest award that the Red Cross gives out.

I have done a lot of bicycle tours since that ride and unfortunately, not all stories about injured riders have a storybook ending like that one. There have been more than a few fatalities on bike rides where I was a medic. Any time you get 2,000 to 5,000 bicyclist riding on American roads day after day, people are going to get killed. There is not much you can say when you let a fact like that settle in your heart. Most medics develop a dark sort of gallows humor as a kind of self-protection.

Here's one of my gallows humor stories:

I was asleep in a gym (where I usually stay) when I woke up to some commotion across the gym. As I was lying there half-awake I heard the words, "Call 911 and get an AED!" I had trained hundreds of CPR students to say those very words.

I immediately jumped up from my bedding on the floor, threw on my summer robe and ran across the gym to assist. We ended up doing CPR on the patient for about twenty minutes until the ambulance showed up. Unfortunately, the fellow did not make it.

It was Day Three of a week-long bike ride, and so even though your patient and fellow bike rider has died, you do the only thing that you and the several thousand other bicyclists can do: you get on your bikes and start riding to the next night's camp.

That next day I was stopped for a long lunch when the woman sitting next to me asked if I was one of the guys in the gym who had worked on the patient the previous night. I replied that I was, and naturally she asked for details. I told her that I really didn't know exactly; that even though I'd been working on the guy, I wasn't family so I hadn't been given any more information other than that he had died.

We sat there in the warm sun for a few more minutes. She got a pirate smile on her face and then she asked, "Do you always just wear a robe when you are doing CPR?" I immediately became embarrassed. I kind of knew what she was referring to. It was true: when I heard "call 911 and get an AED" I jumped up and ran across the gym to assist — with absolutely nothing on but my robe.

When I am on bike rides I tend to sleep in my sleeping bag with as few clothes on as possible. There is a reason for this, and it is not a XXX reason, either.

On about Day Three of multi-day bike rides I'd often notice riders, both men and women, limping and staggering to the aid station. They weren't hung over. They were in pain. By Day Three they'd passed from being mildly irritated in their groin and crotch area to having an ugly wound in the area. This sort of wound was not uncommon after riding a bike up to 7 hours a day, day after day. These folks were coming to the aid station to get Bag Balm. Bag Balm is a petroleum jelly type sort of paste originally formulated to treat irritation on cows' udders. It's also used to treat wounds like this. The stuff is much better than just plain petroleum jelly. I have no idea why it works better but it does. The stuff is amazing.

But to prevent developing wounds like this in the first place, the key is proper hygiene and letting the skin breathe and heal overnight — especially when you are going to be riding a full day the next day. So I've learned to sleep in my sleeping bag with as little on as possible, to keep the irritation under control.

So: Apparently when I was doing CPR my robe had not remained totally closed. There I was, naked under my robe, giving onlookers (and there were about 75 of them) a view of anything they wanted to look at.

The woman was not coming on to me. She was there with her husband. She had simply made me and the people around us laugh at the small humorous sidenote in a tragic incident.

The best medicine is laughter, and it helped. It is always difficult when a fellow rider dies. Her comments helped ease the pain.

And I had been honest in telling her I had no details about what had happened with the rider who died. Frequently, after a patient is put in the ambulance I will never know the outcome, simply because I do not have the right to know. I am not family, and then, of course, there is the whole liability issue. On more than one bike ride I have been very worried about a patient I had treated yet could never find out if they had even lived or died.

Laughter really is the best medicine.

CHAPTER 19

Return To The Scene Of The Crime

I had no desire to return to the Tetons for well over a decade after my accident. That is not to say that I did not still love the place. It was just too painful to go back. For Sharyn, the emotional pain was even worse.

She'd seen the helicopters flying around over the Grand and had asked rangers what had happened. She was told a climber had fallen. She asked, "who"? and added that her friend was climbing The Grand. When the rangers asked who her friend was and she gave them my name, they told her she'd better come with them, and had taken her to the Ranger Station. No one had to draw a map for her. She knew something very bad had happened. And of course that was just the beginning. So going to visit The Tetons to "have a vacation" was about the last thing she wanted to do.

I did not return to the Tetons until over 15 years later. I had become an EMT and was doing my Riding Bicyclist Medic thing. One summer I signed up for a 150-mile Multiple Sclerosis ride leaving from Billings, Montana. I had not done much riding in Montana, so I decided to check it out. It was a good two-day ride and I had a lot of fun. On the way back down to Denver, I dropped into Yellowstone for a couple of hours and then drove on to Jackson. I had my tent with me, so I camped the first night and then stayed three more nights in the Hostel.

I still loved the place! I took one look at The Grand and for the first time since I fell I wanted to climb again. The same ole magic that had attracted me when I was a kid came back with a vengeance. One look at those hills and I was absolutely gripped by them. I still love those hills. Only the Alps come close to holding me so strongly.

I did not try to climb them again.

The Park folks had built a bike path from Jackson out to the ranger station where the climbs begin. I rode out there and strolled into the station. Although it was summer, no one was there but two rangers, so I decided to see if they remembered my fall.

I said I was a climber and that I'd had a serious fall on The Grand back in 1995. That was before his time, the younger ranger said. The second ranger, who looked to be at least my age, asked me some questions about the fall and eventually said he remembered it. Two climbers had fallen, he said. That pretty much confirmed for me that he did remember the incident.

He said they'd heard I had a very serious head injury and that they never really got the lowdown on what happened to me.

So I told him about my recovery. I said it had taken about three years before I'd even come close to being the person I was before the fall. I also mentioned that I'd written the Ranger Staff a letter thanking them for taking care of me. He laughed and said, "We get a lot of those letters."

We chit-chatted some more. I asked him if he participated in my rescue. He had, he said. Apparently, he helped lower me to the saddle between the Middle and Grand Teton where the Exum camp was located. The helicopter crew had met us there and loaded the other climber and me onto the helicopter to take us to Jackson Hospital.

All of this coming together in the ranger station in just a few minutes of casual conservation was a little hard to take. The guys and gals at this ranger station had saved my life! There was no question about it. I told him that I would like to shake his hand and thank him, which I did. He was pleased with that.

It turned out that he was not an official ranger anymore because he had retired. Now he was a volunteer. He did not "run up the mountain" like he used to, he laughed. It was great just hanging out with him.

Eventually I mentioned to him that as a result of my accident I'd decided to become an EMT and was now doing ski patrols as well as working as a medic on bike rides all over the country. I said I'd gotten to "play it forward" and told him about the Ride the Rockies incident. We'd used CPR and AED, I said, and the guy was alive and walking around today. The ranger looked at me and smiled a huge smile. "Feels good, doesn't it?"

"Yes it does!"

I left a few minutes later and walked around the whole area. It had not changed much since I'd visited as a child, which is a good thing!

I biked around Jackson and the Grand Teton National Park a few more days. I met lots of cool folk and drank some really good beer. The tourist towns in Wyoming are in the brewery business big time just like in Colorado. What I was really doing, silly as it may sound, was hanging around until I felt like I had made my peace with the Grand Teton.

After breakfast one morning I just knew: it was time to head home to Colorado. I had made my peace with the hill. I rode by it one last time and the damn thing still just literally reached out and grabbed me. And again the memories and feelings I'd had standing on top of the Grand washed over me — thoughts about my family, my parents, and all that had happened there. I was glad I had come. It was necessary. Now the Tetons were my friend again.

I will probably never climb again but I certainly will go back to The Grand Tetons and ski, skinny ski, hike and ride my bike. We humans often act as though animals and objects are really human, with human intentions and behavior. I know I called the Grand Teton the "Grand Bitch" for years, and so did Sharyn. I still do sometimes. But really I prefer to think that the Grand Bitch saved my life. Yes, she almost killed me, but she did not kill me. I lived. When I fell on The Grand, I was planning a trip to climb some of my favorite mountains in the Alps — the Jungfrau, Mount

Blanc, the Matterhorn. Nothing horribly hard; but then, climbers get killed in the Alps all the time. Europeans do not even make a big deal about the deaths because they happen so frequently. So I prefer to think that really The Grand was taking care of me — giving me a wake-up call to keep me from going to Europe to climb. Thus, actually, she saved my life.

Well, that is what I like to think. I survived a TBI. I can think whatever I want to.

I will be going up to see my old friends The Grand Tetons next summer!

CHAPTER *20*

I Lived — 20 Years Later

Like many important things that eventually happen in life, it just kind of came up one day. I have a group of friends who meet in the morning at our favorite coffee place in the Denver area. On any given day, there are from 10 to 30 of us sitting around talking for a couple of hours before we take off to live the rest of the day. It's a great way to start the day.

I was sitting there with my friends one morning in mid-August and I brought up that it was getting close to my anniversary date for my accident. Most of my friends did not know that I had a mountain climbing accident. We were chit chatting about it and I suddenly realized that this anniversary was going to be the 20th anniversary of the accident: 20 years ago to the day.

Most of my friends were surprised when I described what happened on The Grand Teton. They did not know I'd been a mountain climber, much less that I'd had a "life-altering" fall. They all thought of me as a road bicyclist or a cross-country-alpine skier, which are the sports I've focused on since my recovery.

The good news was that most of them could not tell that I had a TBI.

Even after all that has happened, the TBI is still something I do not usually volunteer. It is not really a secret, but it is not something that usually comes up in routine conversation. Even nice people sometimes tend to judge a TBI survivor.

I still get broken bones, which is just part of the game when you are a very active skier/bicyclist. "Sh*t happens," as they say. Many of my friends at the coffee shop also had accidents and got hurt just like I did. We would often compare injuries and take care of each other and take care of each other's bicycles (which REALLY matters). However, until I'd told them about my TBI they had no idea.

When they found out, of course they started ribbing me: "So that's what's wrong with you!" and "We knew something was wrong!" The bottom line, though, is that most of them had no idea that I had any kind of brain injury until I told them. TBIs are not exactly something you brag about and usually I just kept it to myself. Survivors tend to hide their condition so that no one figures out anything's wrong. I was no exception. Not only did I live but for the most part the TBI was not noticeable. Excellent!

These are very nice and extremely supportive folks. Several said that obviously my accident was a game-changer and that we should have a celebration to mark the anniversary — a celebration of life. After all, they said, it not all that common to run into someone who'd fallen off the Grand Teton and lived to tell about it.

On the actual day of the twentieth anniversary, August 22, 2015, around 30 of my friends bought a really nice cake and showed up in force at the coffee shop. It was a great a celebration.

I tend to divide my life into "before my fall" and "after my fall." Clearly, my fall on August 22, 1995 was/is one of the most significant moments in my life. Nothing was the same after the accident. And this celebration was a necessary step for me in getting on with my life. This anniversary was also when I started writing this book.

CHAPTER 21

Survivors

I wrote this book because I love writing, and I felt a need to write about my accident and recovery. Those of you who are writers know there comes a time when you must put it down on paper or live with a very strong feeling of unfinished business. I needed to put it down on paper.

I also wrote this book for other survivors. This book is for them. It is my attempt to instill hope. If laughter is the best medicine, then hope is the best cure — or the closest thing to a cure.

If I can bring hope to a single person with a TBI who is feeling helpless and angry, feeling hopeless; if this book reaches them and they find that bicycling, writing, making art, working with the disabled — or whatever — works for them, then I've succeeded. If I can reach one person who's had a brain injury and make them realize "I'm still alive, and life is a gift so I'll go live," then this book has been a success!

My tool was the bicycle — and patient care. Yours may be different. But something is waiting for you.

Bicycling is such a healthy sport! I'm still discovering how bicycling itself helps folks with various chronic conditions. Watching those with a love of bicycling deal with their chronic illness is simply moving. On MS rides I watch riders struggling to get onto their bicycles and I see determined people. There are no slackers here. I sometimes see their symptoms — the shaking, spasms and awkwardness — start to ease as soon as they get on their bikes and start riding. You can see it in their faces: "Let's ride!"

Once on an MS ride I witnessed a particularly inspiring woman.

I saw her sitting on the ground close to the finish line. She appeared to be about my age. Attractive, probably middle class. I suspected she had been some sort of professional. Maybe she was a doctor, or a teacher, I thought. Maybe a school principal. Or maybe she'd been a hospital administrator. Or a lawyer. Maybe even something a little more exotic, I speculated — like a writer or filmmaker. The sign she was holding said it all. It read, "Thanks for riding to save my life."

I know this disease well enough to know just how nasty it can be, and how society's prejudice and lack of understanding can put people like her out of a job, no matter how smart, well educated, or qualified she may be.

This was the MS 150 Colorado Bike Ride, and I was a riding medic. The MS 150 is a popular ride in a state that takes its bicycling seriously.

The finish line at the end of the two-day fundraiser is a celebration, with a couple thousand bike riders and their team supporters. Hundreds more people with MS and the families have come to offer their support. Loud music blaring, cowbells clanging, and the master of ceremonies shouting — urging all of us on to the finish. Both sides of the finish line are clogged with people with MS, their families, friends, and supporters.

I've been on these rides a lot, and the scene at the finish line never fails to send a chill down my spine and put a tremendous smile on my face. And more than a few times I've let myself go too, and started screaming along with the rest of them as I ride across the finish line. What's cool about screaming is that everybody screams back. You see, this is a movement. A family of sorts. It's is more than just a cause. It is a true movement. MS kills people. Lots of them. We are fighting to stop it, and this is how we do it. The victories are small, but the finish line is one of those victories. Of course it is a celebration!

A few feet further on, they're handing out medals. Some may think this is trite, but I personally am proud of my MS medals. Most who finish wear their medal around their neck with pride. When I get home, I will pin the medal to my wall along with my Ride the Rockies medic plaques and other medic medals.

After getting my medal and checking in with the lead medic, I ate, then wandered back where I had seen the woman with the sign. She was still there, but she was on the other side of the finish line, and getting to her would have entailed getting through hundreds of onlookers, cars, support vans and 500 or so bicycles. So I just let her physical image be enough. I knew the moment that I saw her and her sign that I would write about her.

Her sign told the truth. It was not an exaggeration. There is no cure for MS. They do not know what causes MS. So the sign is correct. Probably MS will cause her death, directly or indirectly. The disease takes decades off patients' lives.

Her simple sign was correct: How long she lives depends upon MS research — and we, the MS 150 riders, were raising money for that research. Her sign also accurately described the feeling and emotion of the ride. We were riding to save her life, and the lives of all the others with MS.

The more than 90 MS rides nationwide are some of the best bike rides in the country. In general, they're well organized, fun, and safe. As a medic I have had to send riders to the hospital in an ambulance. And I've heard of more extreme cases where patients had to be sent by helicopter to trauma centers. But this kind of thing is going to happen on any ride with thousands of rider. In general MS rides are very safe.

On MS rides, patients with MS get on their bikes and ride. To folks unfamiliar with MS this may not seem big deal. It is a big deal. The effects of the disease itself make it difficult to ride. And sun and exertion can aggravate MS symptoms significantly. Riding long distances is just plain hard — and sometimes dangerous. I watch these riders with MS get on their bikes and ride the distance. Some are showing symptoms of their disease. Some wear a jersey telling us who they are. Others don't. But one thing they have in common is their insistence that they are not going to let MS ruin their lives.

The word "courage" comes to mind. But after decades of work with disabled people, I now understand it as something different. How they say it may vary, but they're saying the same thing: that this goddamn disease is not going to ruin their lives. "I am going to live and if I want to ride my bike to Fort Collins then I am going to ride my bike to Fort Collins and MS is not going to stop me."

These are my patients, and I see things in them that they do not see in themselves.

If these folks were put in charge of stopping climate change in America, it would have been stopped. These folks do not lie to themselves or get sidetracked by propaganda. They are focused, and they do what needs to be done. They do it, no excuses and no whining. They do what must be done and that is it.

There's nothing extravagant, self-serving, or selfish about it. This disease showed up in their bodies uninvited and unwelcome, but it is there and they know it will probably kill them, but these riders with MS have made a decision: they are going to live their lives the way they want to. This is their life and MS is not going to stop it for them. At least not today.

I am proud to be a medic on MS rides. I regret that I didn't ask that woman with the sign to marry me, or at least have a glass of wine. I hope I see her at another MS ride.

Everything I said about MS riders is the same for Tour de Cure riders, Beat Cancer riders, Stop Parkinson's riders — all of them. I feel that the MS story tells it best. The determination and courage of bicycle riders who have serious chronic illnesses is remarkable. The good news is that medicine is discovering that bicycling helps/assists the patients with their symptoms. Frequently, when MS patients start riding their bikes their symptoms seem to disappear or at least diminish while riding.

Medical researchers have discovered that Parkinson's patients also improve when riding. According to research, when the patients get on their bikes and ride for an hour or so, their symptoms will disappear or significantly diminish for several hours after they stop riding. This is no small potatoes. The researchers do not know why this occurs but the evidence that riding a bike will assist in diminishing symptoms in many

Parkinson's patients is clearly a step forward in treatment. Like most of these chronic illnesses Parkinson's is a nasty disease and it takes courage to stand up to it just like MS, Diabetes, TBI, Cancer, etc.

It is for these people/patients — these survivors — that I have written this book. This book is for the patient suffering from a chronic illness that feels their life is over. Your life is not over! RIDE ON! I will see you on your cause's bike ride! You can do it.

Say the words with me: "I choose life — I want to live".

Scott on top of the Grand Teton.

ABOUT THE AUTHOR

Scott Houchin was born and raised in La Grange, Kentucky. During his college years he became an environmental, civil rights, and peace organizer. He later pursued a career in civil rights for over 27 years. He has been climbing, bicycling, hiking, cross country skiing and alpine skiing since he was ten years old. He presently lives in Denver Colorado which is his home base for traveling all over America, Canada, Mexico, and Europe.